POCKET

Remember the excitement of unveiling the secrets within a mini box as a child?

Reconnect with your cherished childhood memories of tiny houses and pocket worlds with this coloring book.

COLOR YOURSELF HAPPY!

In today's demanding world, managing our mental health is vital. Recent years have taken a toll on us, and that's why immersing ourselves in art has become an essential part of our self-care routine, bringing joy and inner peace.

PAPER CHOICE

We choose standard-quality paper for affordability due to the limited paper options on Amazon. You can prevent bleeding that may occur with certain pens or markers by placing a blank sheet of thicker paper behind the page you're coloring. We appreciate your understanding of our paper selection.

SHARE YOUR ARTWORKS

Since launching our Adult Coloring Books on Amazon, we've seen countless pages come to life by creative colorists like you. When you leave a review, feel free to share pictures and celebrate your unique creations. We are excited to see your masterpieces! ☺

CONNECT WITH US

For any concerns, please feel free to contact us at **support@cocowyo.com**

(@cocowyopublishing)

a blank sheet of paper

BEFORE STARTING YOUR COLORING JOURNEY

Amazon's paper is ideal for coloring with colored pencils and alcohol-based markers. Use a blank sheet behind the page for wet mediums to prevent bleed-through.

SHARING, LEARNING AND COLORING TIPS
Visit our Instagram @cocowyopublishing

How I Color MUSHROOM

cocowyopublishing

Cocowyo

- daily coloring tutorial
- artistic guidance
- medium reviews

Follow   Message   Email

Scan me for more fun!

How I Color WATER DROPLETS

How I Color ROSE

50+ FREE DIGITAL COLORING PAGES!

Thank you for choosing our book!
Visit the "Coco Wyo Coloring Books" Facebook group
to download them now!

Share your fabulous finished artwork with us!
Join our Facebook group to let your creativity shine.
Scan the QR code to join the group:

@cocowyopublishing

Coco Wyo Publishing

THIS BOOK
BELONGS TO

_____

_____

TEST COLOR PAGE

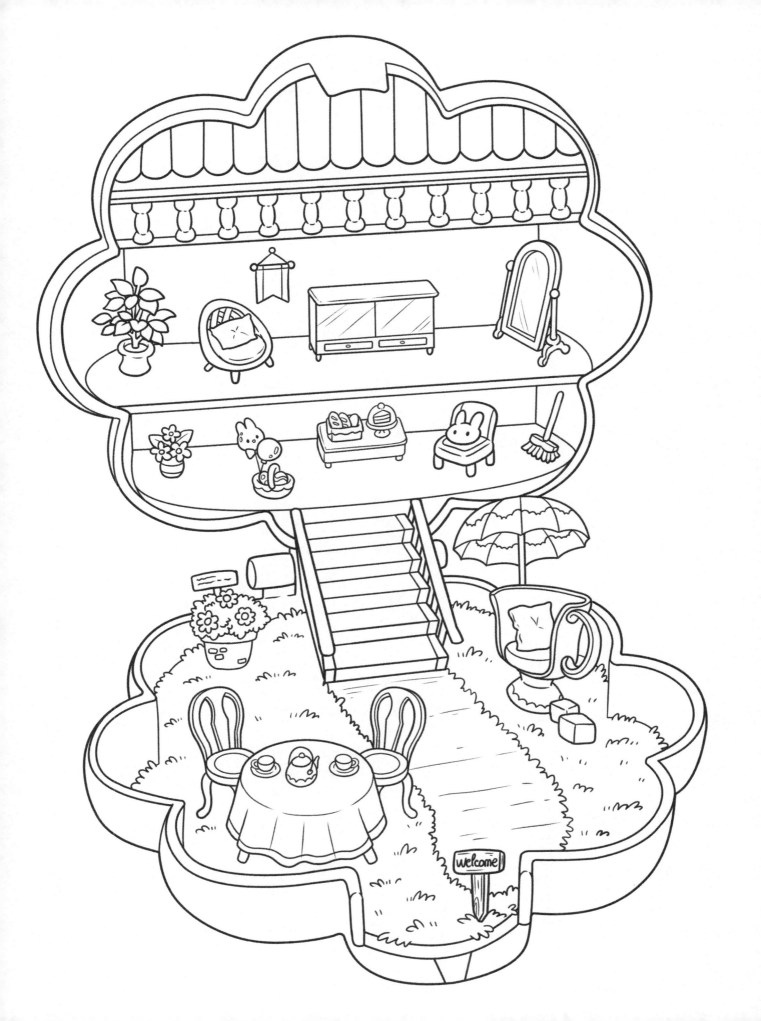

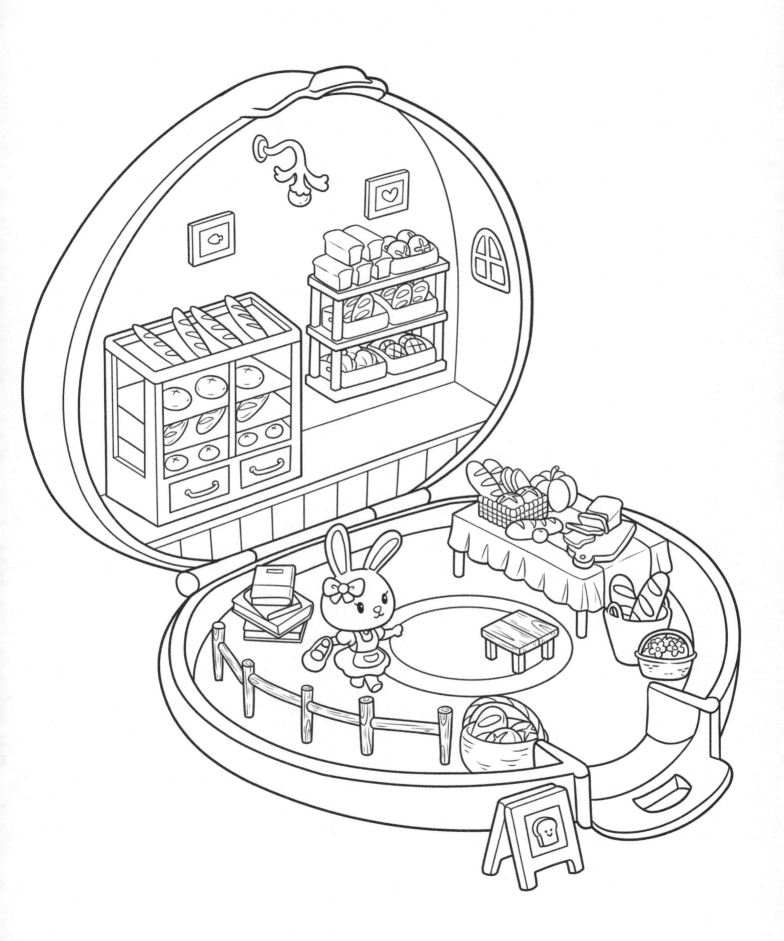

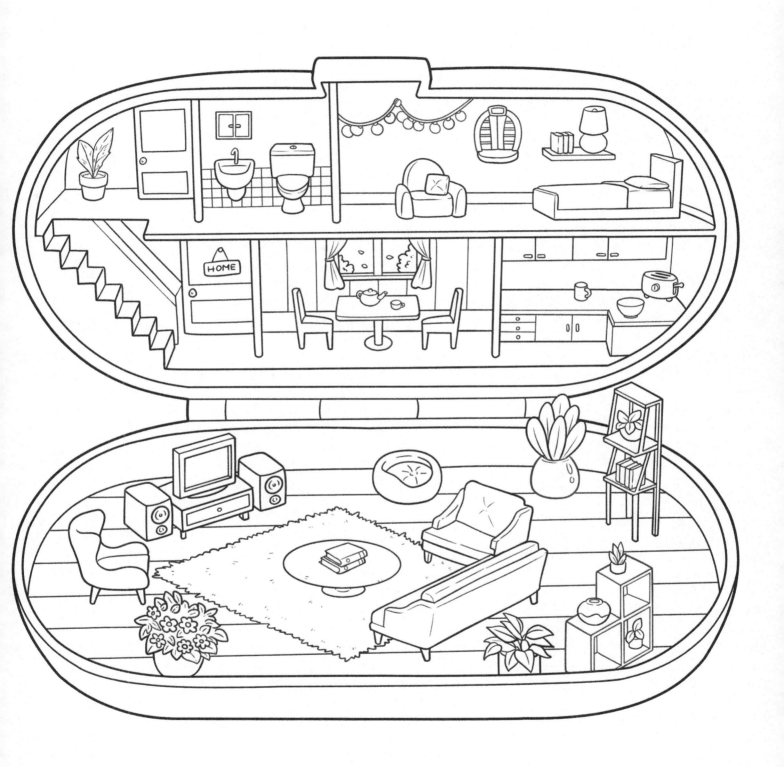

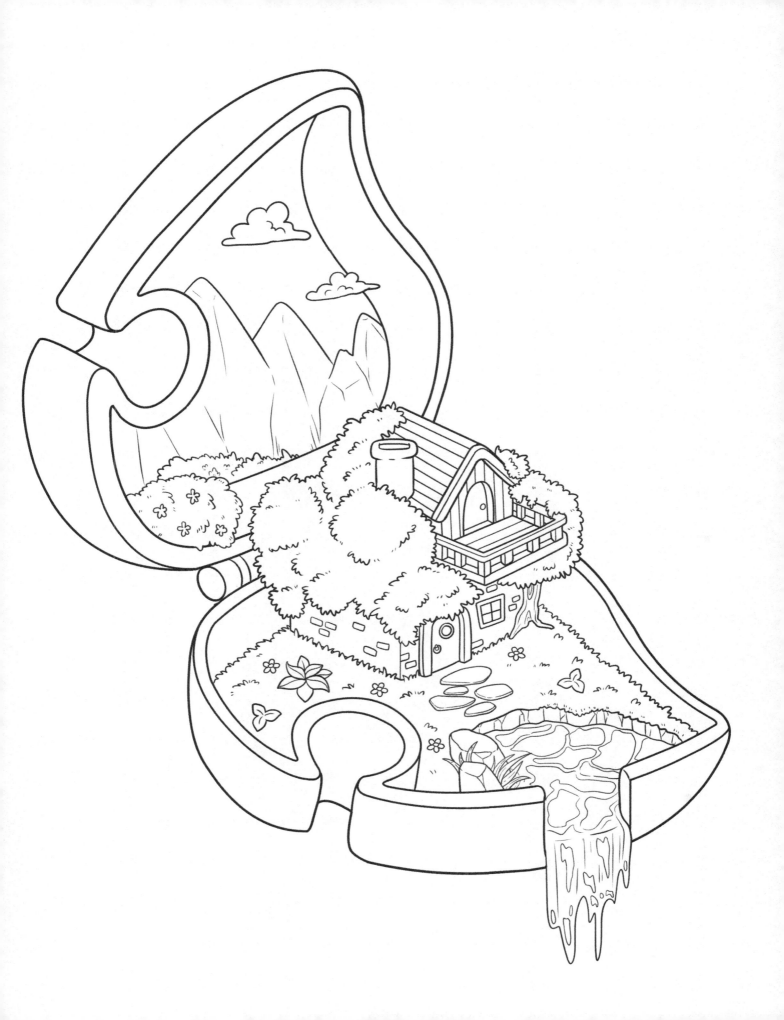

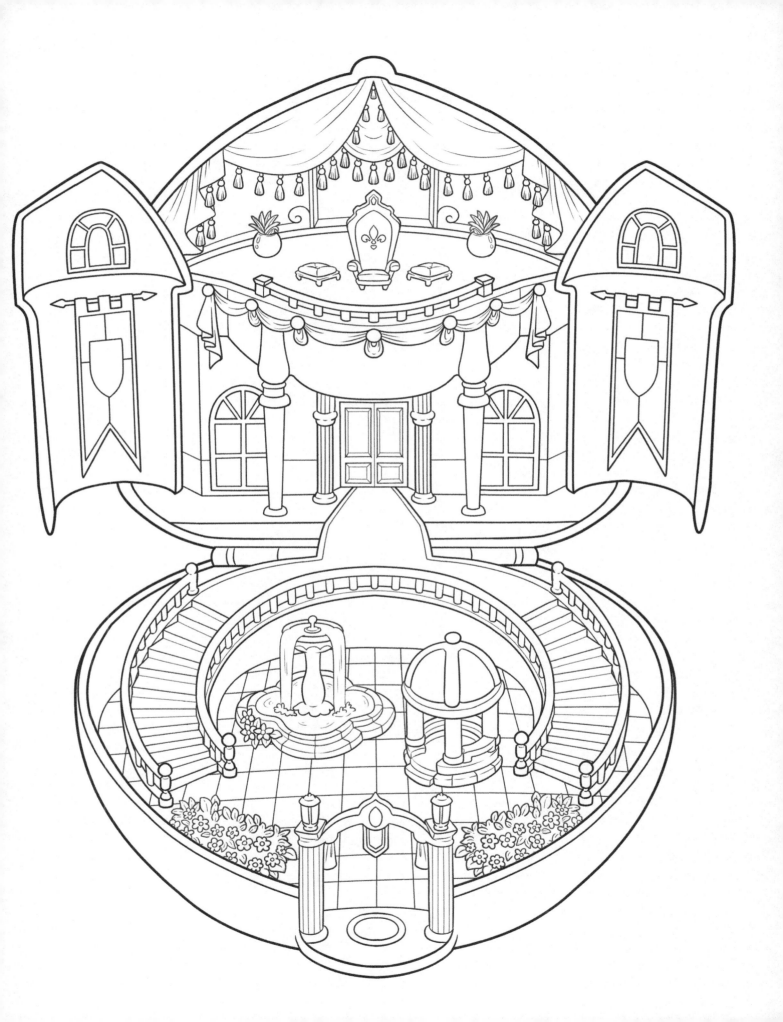

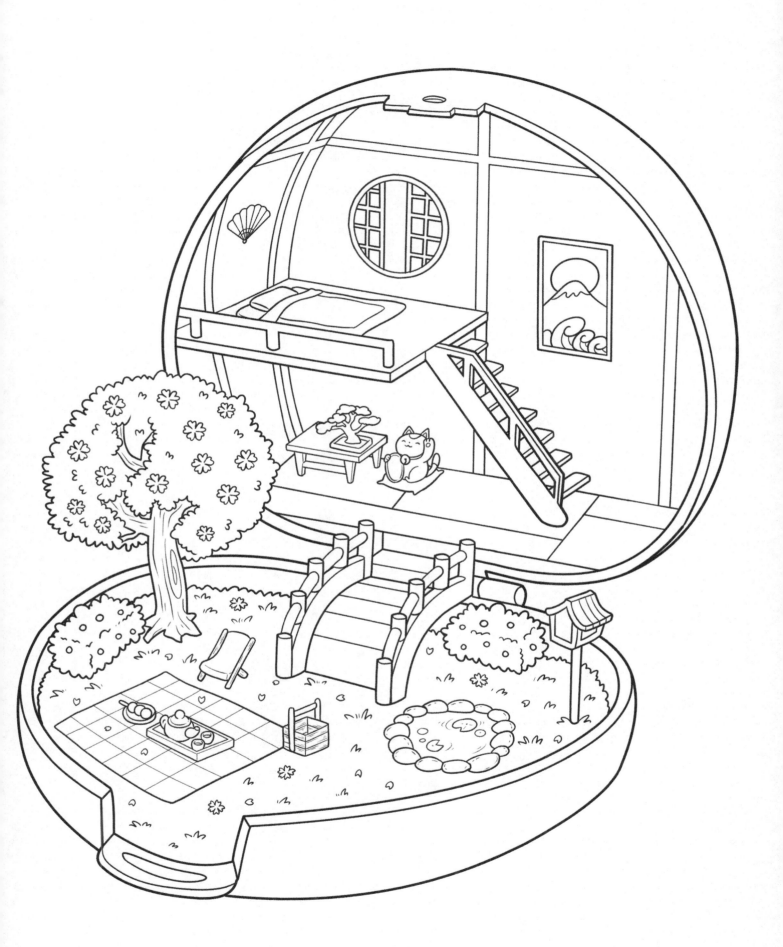

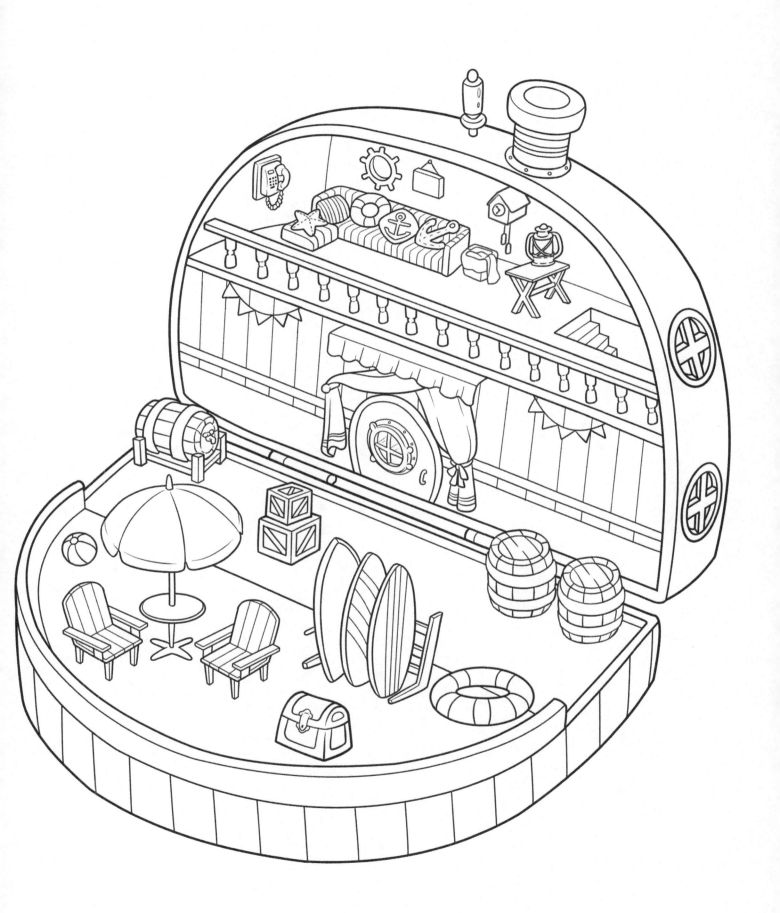

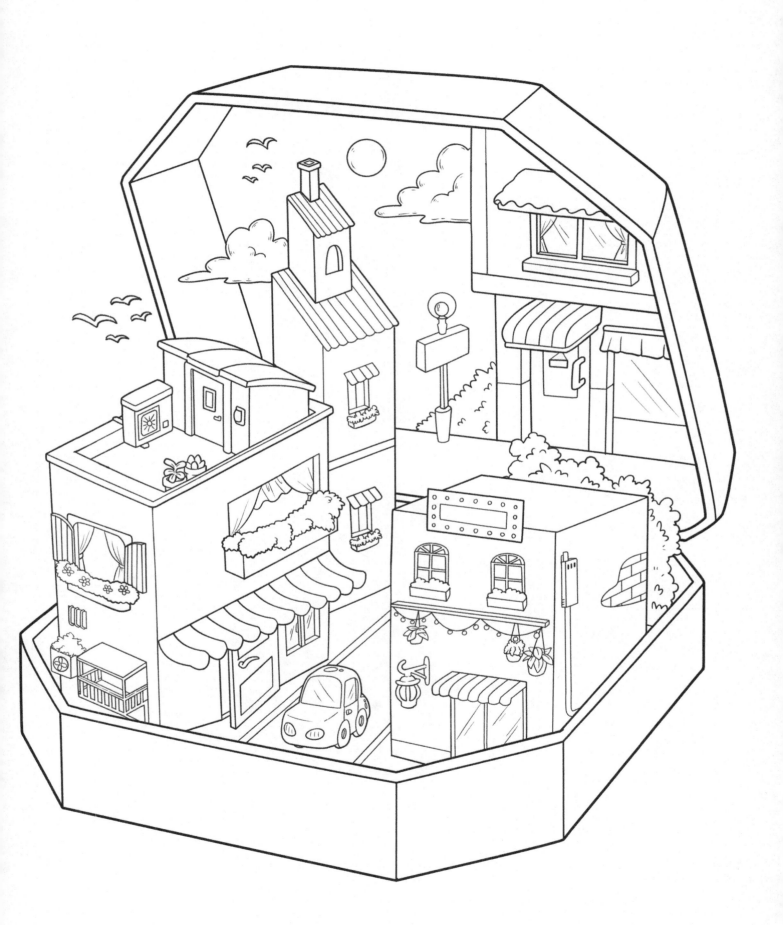

Made in the USA
Coppell, TX
19 May 2024

31818640R30050